SOUTH CAROLINA GAMECOCKS

BY JEFF SEIDEL

SportsZone

An Imprint of Abdo Publishing
abdopublishing.com

abdopublishing.com

Published by Abdo Publishing, a division of ABDO, PO Box 398166, Minneapolis, Minnesota 55439.

Printed in the United States of America, North Mankato, Minnesota
052018
092018

THIS BOOK CONTAINS RECYCLED MATERIALS

Cover Photo: Wade Payne/AP Images
Interior Photos: Wade Payne/AP Images, 1; Al Messerschmidt/Getty Images Sport/Getty Images, 4–5, 6, 43 (bottom right); Mary Ann Chastain/AP Images, 9; Reid Compton/Icon SMI ARA/Newscom, 11; Streeter Lecka/Getty Images Sport/Getty Images, 12–13, 43 (top right); Collegiate Images/Getty Images, 15, 18–19, 26–27, 42 (left), 43 (top left); Jim Dedmon/Icon Sportswire, 21, 44; Jamie Lamor Thompson/Shutterstock Images, 24; Dave Pickoff/AP Images, 28; John Iacono/Sports Illustrated/Getty Images, 31; Ric Feld/AP Images, 32, 42 (right); John Raoux/AP Images, 34–35, 43 (bottom left); Steve Jacobson/Sports Illustrated Classic/Getty Images, 37; Sean Rayford/AP Images, 39; Margaret Bowles/AP Images, 40

Editor: Patrick Donnelly
Series Designer: Craig Hinton

Library of Congress Control Number: 2017962093

Publisher's Cataloging-in-Publication Data

Names: Seidel, Jeff, author.
Title: South Carolina Gamecocks / by Jeff Seidel.
Description: Minneapolis, Minnesota : Abdo Publishing, 2019. | Series: Inside college football | Includes online resources and index.
Identifiers: ISBN 9781532114601 (lib.bdg.) | ISBN 9781532154430 (ebook)
Subjects: LCSH: American football--Juvenile literature. | College sports--United States--History--Juvenile literature. | University of South Carolina. Fighting Gamecocks--Juvenile literature. | Football--Records--United States--Juvenile literature.
Classification: DDC 796.332630--dc23

TABLE OF CONTENTS

Wide receiver Alshon Jeffery runs in for the touchdown against Alabama in 2010.

1

DIVISION CHAMPIONS

STEVE SPURRIER WON THE HEISMAN TROPHY AS A QUARTERBACK AT THE UNIVERSITY OF FLORIDA. HE ALSO WON A NATIONAL CHAMPIONSHIP THERE AS HEAD COACH. BUT ONE OF HIS TOUGHEST JOBS WAS TURNING SOUTH CAROLINA INTO A WINNER.

Spurrier took over as the Gamecocks' head coach in 2005. South Carolina wasn't a traditional power by any means. Its only conference championship in football came in 1969 in the Atlantic Coast Conference (ACC). Spurrier faced an uphill battle to turn the program around in the rugged Southeastern Conference (SEC).

But by 2010 he had built a team that he thought was a winner. The Gamecocks opened SEC play with a 17–6 win over 22nd-ranked Georgia. A 35–27 loss at Auburn was a setback. But the Gamecocks were ready when No. 1 Alabama visited Columbia, South Carolina.

Quarterback Stephen Garcia prepares to pass against the Crimson Tide.

South Carolina had played Alabama three times before. The Gamecocks were 0–3 in those games. But none of that mattered to the fans who packed Williams-Brice Stadium on October 9, 2010. The crowd went wild as the 19th-ranked Gamecocks ran onto the field. Then their roars shook the stadium as the home team raced to a 21–3 lead.

Alabama's fans were stunned into silence. They were used to seeing their Crimson Tide roll over their opponents. Alabama was the defending national champion and riding a 19-game winning streak. That year's team featured a number of future National Football League (NFL) stars. Junior running back Mark Ingram had won the Heisman Trophy a year earlier. Wide receiver Julio Jones would be the sixth pick in the NFL Draft the next spring. Four defensive starters would go on to be first-round picks. Alabama was loaded with talent.

But South Carolina had a few weapons of its own. Freshman running back Marcus Lattimore was heading for a 1,000-yard season. Wide receiver Alshon Jeffery would lead the SEC with 88 catches and 1,517 receiving yards. Quarterback Stephen Garcia seemed to come up with a big play whenever the Gamecocks needed it most.

Garcia threw a touchdown pass to Lattimore and two more to Jeffery and the Gamecocks led by 18 points early in the second quarter. Alabama tried to rally, but the Tide never got closer than a touchdown. Lattimore scored on two short runs in the second half, the latter sealing a 35–21 victory.

It was the type of victory that helped Spurrier make his name as a big-time coach at Florida. Spurrier was head coach there from 1990 to 2001. He led the Gators to the national title in 1996.

A QUICK STUDY

Stephon Gilmore graduated from high school in December 2008, a half-year before his classmates. He had earned a scholarship to South Carolina and wanted to join the Gamecocks for practice as early as he could. His efforts paid off handsomely. Gilmore started all 13 games at cornerback for South Carolina that fall. It's rare that a true freshman is given that type of responsibility in the SEC. But Gilmore was a rare talent. He was named to three Freshman All-America teams that year. He went on to start every game the next two years as well, leading the team in interceptions both years. His solid play anchored the Gamecocks' defensive backfield. It also drew the attention of NFL scouts. The Buffalo Bills chose Gilmore with the 10th pick of the 2011 NFL Draft.

Spurrier left Florida for an offer to coach in the NFL. But he lasted just two years as the head coach in Washington. Before long, he was back in the SEC, taking the South Carolina job in 2005. He never quite pushed the Gamecocks up to the level Florida had reached. But South Carolina had a season to remember in 2010. Another huge moment that year took place in Spurrier's old home.

TOO MANY INJURIES

Marcus Lattimore was considered a future star running back in the NFL during his days at South Carolina. But a series of knee injuries suffered while playing for the Gamecocks proved too much for him to overcome.

In 2011 Lattimore's season ended after just seven games when he tore a ligament in his knee in a game at Mississippi State. He worked hard to rehab the injury. When he came back as a junior, he was determined to show he was fully recovered.

But then disaster struck. In a game against Tennessee in late October, Lattimore suffered a gruesome injury on a low tackle by a defender. The hit dislocated Lattimore's right kneecap and tore every ligament in the knee.

Despite those injuries, the San Francisco 49ers selected him in the fourth round of the 2013 NFL Draft. The running back spent the 2013 season on the NFL's non-football injury list trying to work his way back into shape. But midway through the 2014 season, Lattimore accepted that his knee was too badly damaged to continue. He decided to retire. But Lattimore's football days were not over. In 2018 Gamecocks coach Will Muschamp hired Lattimore to serve as the team's director of player development for life skills.

Marcus Lattimore scored 19 touchdowns his freshman year.

The Gamecocks' final SEC game of the season had a lot on the line. The winner would be the champion of the SEC Eastern Division and earn a spot in the SEC title game. And of course, Spurrier wanted to show his old fans that he had built another championship-caliber team.

Florida struck first as Andre Debose returned the opening kickoff 99 yards for a touchdown. Just 14 seconds in, the Gators led 7–0. But it

THE GAME BALL

Many football teams give out game balls after victories. The recipients are usually players. Sometimes they'll go to a coach who played a big part in that week's game plan. And when the Gamecocks beat No. 1 Alabama in 2010, coach Steve Spurrier knew who to reward. "I gave myself a game ball for that one," he told the media after the 35–21 victory.

was all South Carolina from that point on. Lattimore was the focus of the offensive attack that day. He carried the ball 40 times for 212 yards. He also scored three touchdowns. Kicker Spencer Lanning booted three field goals. Florida tried to claw its way back with a fourth-quarter touchdown. But Lattimore iced the win with an 11-yard touchdown run. Several of his teammates pushed the pile to help him across the goal line.

After the 36–14 victory, Spurrier joked about coming up with the big win at Florida's home stadium, which is nicknamed "the Swamp." The motto there is "Where only Gators get out alive." Spurrier twisted that phrase a bit when his Gamecocks scored the division-clinching victory. He told the media, "Sometimes the Gamecocks get out alive."

It was South Carolina's second win in 10 tries at the Swamp since joining the SEC. It also earned the Gamecocks a trip to the SEC title game. Two weeks later, they whipped in-state rival Clemson 29–7 in their regular-season finale, but that was the last of their victories that year. The Gamecocks lost to Auburn for the second time that season in the SEC title game. Tigers quarterback Cam Newton accounted for six touchdowns in a 56–17 victory for the eventual national champions.

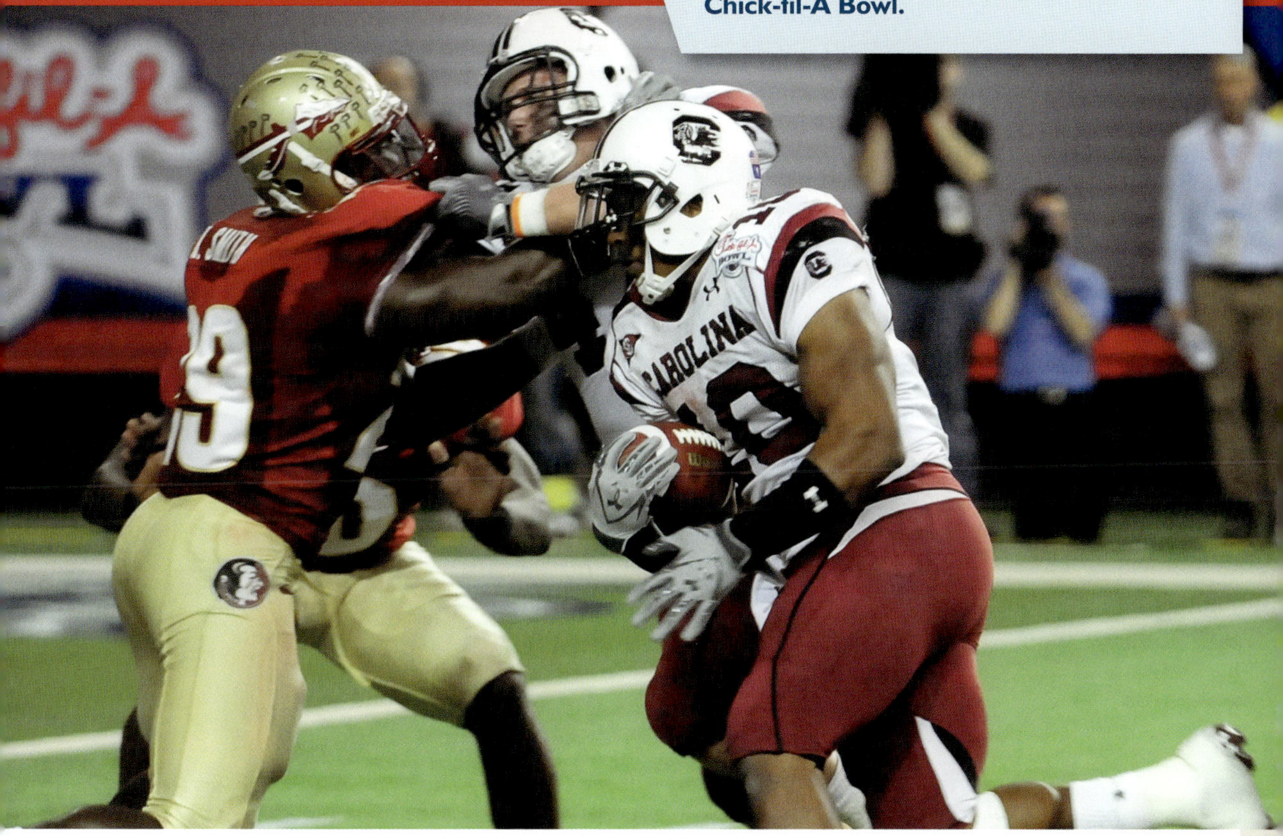

Running back Brian Maddox heads toward the goal line in the Chick-fil-A Bowl.

Then in the Chick-fil-A Bowl against Florida State, the Gamecocks lost Lattimore early due to a concussion after a big hit. The standout freshman carried the ball just one time in the game. His absence was a big reason why Florida State handed the Gamecocks a 26–17 loss.

It wasn't the way the Gamecocks had envisioned their season ending. But their performance in 2010 was the first sign that Spurrier had built a program that could compete in the tough SEC.

The Gamecocks run onto the field at Williams-Brice Stadium amid cheers from fans.

2

THE EARLY DAYS

THE SOUTH CAROLINA FOOTBALL PROGRAM BEGAN IN 1892. BUT SOUTH CAROLINA WASN'T MUCH OF A FACTOR IN THE EARLY DAYS OF COLLEGE FOOTBALL. IN FACT, IN 1906 THE TRUSTEES AT THE SCHOOL BANNED THE SPORT. THEY REPORTEDLY OBJECTED TO THE ROWDY BEHAVIOR OF THE FANS ATTENDING GAMES. HOWEVER, THE BAN LASTED JUST ONE YEAR. THE FOOTBALL TEAM WAS BACK IN 1907. BUT THE GAMECOCKS DIDN'T REALLY MAKE A SPLASH UNTIL THEY JOINED THE SOUTHERN CONFERENCE IN 1922.

At the time, the Southern Conference included many of the teams that now play in the SEC and the ACC. South Carolina was already playing most of them on a regular basis. So it made sense to make it official by joining the conference.

By 1932 the conference had grown to 23 schools. That made it difficult to manage. The next year, many of the stronger teams split off to form the SEC. And in 1933 the Gamecocks made their first bid for a conference title.

They finished 6–3–1 overall and 3–0 against opponents from the new 10-team Southern Conference. But Duke ended up 4–0 in conference play that season, giving the Blue Devils the league title.

The Gamecocks made their first appearance in a bowl game after the 1945 season. They were invited to play in the first Gator Bowl. It took place in Jacksonville, Florida, on January 1, 1946. The Gamecocks were invited despite having finished the regular season with a 2–3–3 record. The Gator Bowl organizers hoped having local teams in the game would help sell tickets for the first-time event. Also, South Carolina head coach Rex Enright was wrapping up a three-year military leave. He was stationed near Jacksonville.

South Carolina's Gator Bowl opponent was a familiar one. Wake Forest also played in the Southern Conference. The teams had played to a 13–13 tie late in the regular season. In the rematch, the Gamecocks took a 7–6 lead into halftime behind a 1-yard touchdown run by Bobby Giles and a Dutch Brembs extra point kick. But the game belonged to Wake Forest after that. Dick Brinkley scored two touchdowns and Bob Smathers added one more. That pushed Wake Forest's lead to 26–7.

THE NICKNAME

South Carolina is the lone major athletic program in the United States that uses "Gamecocks" as its official nickname and mascot. The morning newspaper in Columbia came up with the nickname in 1903 and it stuck.

Brembs struck back for the Gamecocks with a 90-yard interception return for a touchdown. He also kicked

Gamecocks running back King Dixon takes a hit during a 1957 game.

the extra point. But South Carolina could do no more. Wake Forest posted a 26–14 victory.

The Gamecocks finished with just 157 yards of total offense as Wake Forest pushed them around the whole game. The bowl game was the last game for Johnnie McMillan as the head coach. Enright, who had coached the team from 1938 to 1942, returned to the helm in 1946. He stayed on for another 10 years. Through the end of the 2017 season, Enright still had coached the most games at South Carolina. He finished with a 64–69–7 record in 140 games. His 64 wins rank second in school history behind the 86 posted by Steve Spurrier in 135 games.

Enright oversaw another conference switch for South Carolina. The Southern Conference rebounded quickly after the loss of the SEC teams. Membership ballooned to 17 teams by the late 1940s. So in 1953, seven of those schools split off to form the ACC. The Gamecocks joined Clemson, Duke, Maryland, North Carolina, North Carolina State, and Wake Forest as ACC charter members.

WILLIAMS-BRICE STADIUM

The Gamecocks play home games in Williams-Brice Stadium in Columbia. Originally known as Carolina Stadium, it opened during the 1934 season with a capacity of 17,600. Since the Gamecocks first began to play there, the school has expanded its seating capacity several times. The stadium now seats 80,250 fans.

South Carolina changed the name of the facility to Williams-Brice Stadium in 1972. The name honors the contributions from the estate of Martha Williams-Brice that helped expand the stadium. Williams-Brice's husband, Thomas H. Brice, played on the South Carolina football team from 1922 to 1924.

Williams-Brice Stadium is located about one mile (1.6 km) off the school's campus in Columbia. It's near the South Carolina State Fairgrounds as well as the State Farmers Market. It was one of two stadiums used in the filming of the 1993 movie *The Program*, the story of a fictional college football team.

The Gamecocks still were not able to do much in their first 15 years of ACC membership. Their record generally hovered around .500 with Warren Giese and Marvin Bass each serving five years as head coach. Hoping to make a splash, South Carolina handed the reins to Paul Dietzel in 1966.

Dietzel had won a national championship at Louisiana State University (LSU). He coached at Army back when it still had a dominant program. South Carolina fans hoped Dietzel could be the man to put their team over the top. And though he went just 1–9 in his first year, Gamecocks fans would soon get their wish.

HONORING 'THE CADILLAC'

Steve Wadiak was one of the top running backs in college football in 1950. The South Carolina junior rushed for 998 yards in 10 games that season. The highlight was a 256-yard performance in a 14–14 tie with archrival Clemson. The man they called "The Cadillac" earned All-American honors and was the Southern Conference Player of the Year.

Despite being slowed by an injury as a senior, Wadiak still was named to the Associated Press' All-Southern team. The Pittsburgh Steelers selected him with the 30th pick of the 1952 NFL Draft. However, Wadiak never got to play in the NFL. He was killed in a car crash on March 9, 1952. The Gamecocks retired his No. 37, the first player so honored by the program.

Paul Dietzel watches his team play during a 1970 game.

3

A VERY GOOD YEAR

OVER THE YEARS, SOUTH CAROLINA'S FOOTBALL PROGRAM HAS PRODUCED NUMEROUS GREAT PLAYERS. MANY NOTABLE COACHES HAVE PROWLED THE SIDELINES IN COLUMBIA. FANS HAVE ENJOYED THOUSANDS OF TREASURED MEMORIES ALONG THE WAY. BUT THE 1969 GAMECOCKS REMAIN THE ONLY FOOTBALL TEAM IN SCHOOL HISTORY TO WIN A CONFERENCE CHAMPIONSHIP.

Going into the 1969 season it had been nine years since the Gamecocks had posted a winning record. They had gone 4–6 in 1968, Paul Dietzel's third year as head coach. However, that team had won four of its seven ACC games. That might have been an indication of future success. In fact, many years later, some of those Gamecocks said that a game in 1968 may have laid the foundation for what happened in 1969.

South Carolina ended its 1968 season with its traditional game against in-state rival Clemson. The game meant little to the Gamecocks' bowl hopes, which had long since been dashed. But the players remembered how Clemson's 23–12 victory a year earlier had left a bad taste in their mouths. Determined to do better in 1968, the Gamecocks instead could not do much on offense and trailed 3–0 late in the game.

That's when sophomore defensive back Tyler Hellams scored on a 73-yard punt return. South Carolina held on for a 7–3 victory. "We thought after that, 1969 would be a good year for us," Hellams said.

Dietzel already knew a thing or two about what goes into a good year for a college football team. He had guided LSU to a national championship in 1958. He also coached under legends such as Sid Gillman at Cincinnati, Bear Bryant at Kentucky, and Army's Earl Blaik. Dietzel knew football and how to get things done.

He also took on the role of South Carolina's athletic director when he arrived in 1966. The first time Dietzel met with the team on the practice field, he talked about what he wanted to build in Columbia.

PALMETTO BOWL

South Carolina is called the Palmetto State, and the annual football game between its two biggest universities—South Carolina and Clemson—is known as the Palmetto Bowl. The winner takes home a trophy featuring a palmetto tree. Before 1960 the game was always played on a Thursday night in Columbia. Since then it has been held on campus sites with each team hosting in alternating years. The teams have met every year since 1909, the second-longest continuous rivalry in the nation. The Gamecocks won five straight from 2009 to 2013, but Clemson's 34–10 victory in 2017 gave the Tigers a 69–40–4 overall lead in the series.

The South Carolina marching band opened the Palmetto Bowl in 2015.

One of his ideas was a dorm just for athletes. As he pointed to where he thought would be a good location for it, a huge bolt of lightning flashed in the sky. Then came some loud thunder. It's fair to say Dietzel's days at South Carolina got off to an interesting start.

The Gamecocks had been to just one bowl game ever before the 1969 season. They certainly weren't expecting to buck that trend. But the 1969 season was one of those years when the Gamecocks caught enough breaks to win in many different ways. As the saying goes, the ball kept bouncing their way.

For example, five of their six ACC games were at home that year, including the season opener against Duke. Warren Muir, the Gamecocks' top running back that season, finished off a late drive with a 2-yard touchdown run. That gave the Gamecocks a 27–20 victory. South Carolina needed to score two touchdowns in the final 12 minutes to pull out the win.

The next week, South Carolina clung to a one-point lead against North Carolina. Quarterback Tommy Suggs threw a pass in the direction of wide receiver Fred Zeigler in the end zone. Zeigler was covered by two defenders. North Carolina's Rusty Galbraith deflected the pass. But Zeigler was able to tip the ball and then grab it for a touchdown. That locked up a 14–6 victory over the Tar Heels.

The next week, No. 7 Georgia smashed the Gamecocks 41–16 in a nonconference game. But the Gamecocks bounced back the next week against North Carolina State. Jim Mitchell scored on a 72-yard punt return that helped South Carolina to a 21–16 victory. The Gamecocks were 3–0 in ACC play. The conference schedule featured just six games, and the players began to realize that they might be halfway to history. "We thought, 'Hey, this is something special,'" Suggs said. "We've got three (ACC wins) and three more to go."

The next week, the Gamecocks coughed up a late lead at nonconference foe Virginia Tech. But Suggs and Zeigler teamed up to drive the offense into field goal range. Then Billy DuPre kicked a 47-yard field goal to give South Carolina a 17–16 win.

A 17–0 win over Maryland ran the Gamecocks' ACC record to 4–0. Road losses at Florida State and Tennessee—both nonconference games—set up one of South Carolina's biggest tests of the season.

And on a cold, sleeting day in Winston-Salem, North Carolina, the Gamecocks rose to the occasion.

The defense forced Wake Forest into nine turnovers. Suggs threw three touchdown passes, and South Carolina cruised to a 24–6 victory. After the game, news arrived that North Carolina had beat Clemson. That clinched the ACC championship for South Carolina.

The Gamecocks had already accepted an invitation to the Peach Bowl before they wrapped up the regular season against Clemson. No matter—they won anyway, 27–13, to complete the season 6–0 in ACC play.

EXPANDING THE STADIUM

South Carolina slowly began to improve in the years following the 1969 championship season. Paul Dietzel, who was also the athletic director, wanted to change things in the athletic department. He wanted the Gamecocks' programs to grow. He also wanted to show his football team how much their success meant to the overall athletic program.

"After one of our practices . . . Dietzel had us take a quick shower and took us to a meeting," running back Warren Muir said. "We went into this conference room, and he pulled back a sheet over a table that had a replica of the stadium and the changes he was planning. He told us, 'All the progress we've made, the ticket sales going up—you guys contributed to that, so I wanted to share with you what we're planning to do, the expansion of the stadium. You guys can take credit for that."

The Gamecocks mascot, Cocky, was created in 1980.

The season ended on a bad note against West Virginia on a rainy, cold day in Atlanta. The Peach Bowl turned into a mud bowl, and South Carolina finally got a bad break, as Suggs, limited by the flu, and Zeigler could not do much. The Gamecocks' struggling offense finished with only 190 yards in a 14–3 loss.

Today, aluminum letters three feet (0.9 m) high hang on a wall in the south end zone of Williams-Brice Stadium. They remind fans the Gamecocks were the ACC champs in 1969. It's been a source of pride, though one mixed with a bit of disappointment. "It's real special, but I wish it wasn't," Suggs said in 2009. "I wish we had 20 [conference] titles."

PAPER CHAMPIONS

The National Collegiate Athletic Association (NCAA) used to decide its Division I national championship on paper, not on the field. Media organizations and coaching associations once conducted polls of their members to determine the national champion. Whichever team got the most votes would be declared the champion by each organization. That often led to split championships when one team didn't win every poll. In 1992 the NCAA began taking steps to ensure that the No. 1 and No. 2 teams would face off in a bowl game to determine the national title on the field. This move eventually resulted in the College Football Playoff, which now slots the top four teams in the country in two national semifinal games played at major bowl sites. The winners then meet in the national title game.

Tailback George Rogers squeezes through an opening between defenders in a 1980 game.

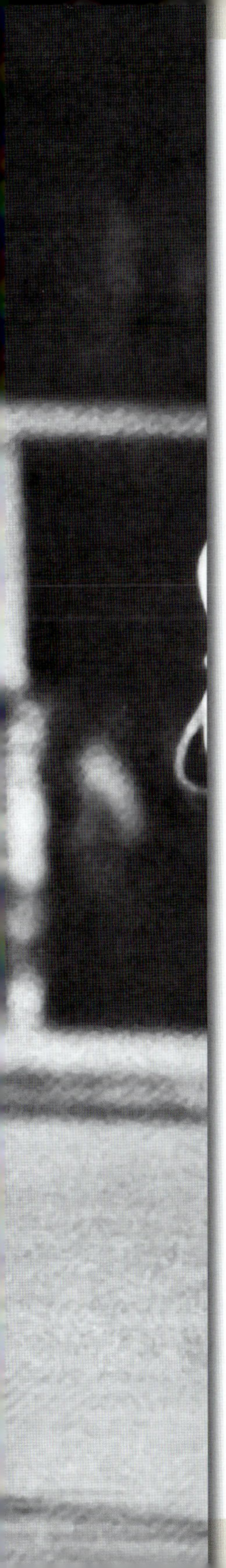

4

BUILDING THE PROGRAM

AFTER WINNING THE ACC TITLE IN 1969, THE GAMECOCKS STUCK AROUND IN THE CONFERENCE FOR JUST ONE MORE YEAR. PAUL DIETZEL AND SOUTH CAROLINA MEN'S BASKETBALL COACH FRANK MCGUIRE HAD GROWN DISGRUNTLED WITH THE ACC. THEY BELIEVED THE FOUR NORTH CAROLINA SCHOOLS—WAKE FOREST, NORTH CAROLINA, NORTH CAROLINA STATE, AND DUKE—HAD TOO MUCH POWER. THE COACHES ALSO THOUGHT THE ACC SET UNREALISTIC ACADEMIC STANDARDS, MAKING IT DIFFICULT TO RECRUIT THE BEST ATHLETES IN THE REGION.

So in 1971, the Gamecocks officially became an independent team. They still played many of their ACC rivals. But their independent status allowed them to expand their search for opponents. By the end of the decade, South Carolina's schedule regularly contained a mix of ACC, SEC, and independent teams.

Another change took place when Dietzel stepped down after the 1974 season. He was replaced by Jim Carlen,

Rogers is all smiles after winning the 1980 Heisman Trophy.

who was on the opposite sideline coaching West Virginia against the Gamecocks in the 1969 Peach Bowl. In seven years, Carlen took South Carolina to three bowl games, one more than the school had been to in its history before his arrival. He left his mark on the program in another way, as well. He convinced George Rogers to become a Gamecock.

Standing 6 feet, 2 inches tall and weighing 220 pounds, Rogers might have been seen as a fullback by other coaches. He would have spent much of his time blocking for a smaller, speedier tailback. But Carlen had other ideas. Graduation had left the Gamecocks short at tailback when Rogers was a freshman in 1977. Carlen put his faith in Rogers, giving him plenty of playing time to showcase his speed and power. He finished with 623 rushing yards, good for second on the squad. And the numbers kept going up from there.

BREAKING THROUGH

Bowl losses became something of a theme for South Carolina. Joe Morrison led the Gamecocks back to the Gator Bowl in 1987 and the Liberty Bowl in 1988 but lost both games. That left South Carolina with an all-time 0–8 in bowl games. Finally, under first-year head coach Brad Scott, the 1994 Gamecocks beat West Virginia 24–21 in the Carquest Bowl on New Year's Day 1995, ending that dubious streak.

Rogers rushed for 1,006 yards in his sophomore season despite splitting time with another back, Johnnie Wright. The next year, Rogers broke out with 1,681 rushing yards and eight touchdowns. He earned All-America honors in the process.

As a senior in 1980, Rogers made history. He rushed for 100 yards in all 12 games that season. That stretched his overall streak to 21 straight 100-yard games. And he did it on some of the biggest stages in college football. When the Gamecocks traveled across the country to face the University of Southern California (USC), Rogers ran for 141 yards. He improved that mark by a yard the next week as the Gamecocks beat Michigan before more than 100,000 fans at "The Big House," Michigan's

STERLING SHARPE

Wide receiver Sterling Sharpe was No. 2 in the program. But he was No. 1 in South Carolina record books after his four years in Columbia. Sharpe ended his career in 1987 as the Gamecocks' all-time leader with 169 receptions, 2,497 receiving yards, and 17 touchdown catches. Alshon Jeffery now holds all three of those records. But Sharpe is the only South Carolina player to have his jersey retired while he was still playing. Sharpe's No. 2 was retired in a ceremony at the end of the 1987 regular season but before the Gamecocks played in the Gator Bowl.

massive home stadium. Rogers also put up 168 yards in a 13–10 loss between the hedges at Georgia.

Rogers finished the regular season with 1,781 rushing yards—tops in the nation—plus 14 touchdowns as South Carolina ended with an 8–3 record. He was a consensus All-America pick and won the Heisman Trophy. He is the only Gamecock to be honored as the best college football player in the nation. The New Orleans Saints chose Rogers with the first overall pick in the NFL Draft.

Carlen stepped down after the 1981 season. His defensive coordinator, Richard Bell, replaced him as head coach but lasted just one year, losing his job after a disappointing 4–7 season. Joe Morrison then arrived in 1983, fresh off a 10-win season at New Mexico.

Morrison was a former star receiver in the NFL whose number was retired by the New York Giants. His second year in Columbia will be remembered for a long time. The Gamecocks won their first nine games. They beat national power programs such as Notre Dame, Pittsburgh,

Sterling Sharpe runs down the field at Williams-Brice Stadium during a 1987 game.

Georgia, and Florida State. South Carolina climbed to No. 2 in the national rankings, its highest mark in school history. But a stunning loss at Navy ended any hopes of a national title. The disappointed Gamecocks rebounded to beat Clemson 22–21 before losing to Oklahoma State 21–14 in the Gator Bowl. They finished the year ranked No. 11 in the country.

Morrison was named the national coach of the year by the Walter Camp Foundation. But his time in Columbia would end in tragedy. In February 1989, coming off consecutive 8–4 seasons, Morrison suffered a fatal heart attack while playing racquetball. He was just 51 years old.

Lou Holtz was the Gamecocks' head coach from 1999 to 2004.

The Gamecocks joined the SEC when it expanded in 1991. The rugged conference proved to be a tough test, and it took some time before South Carolina was competitive again. A 1–10 finish in 1998 cost Brad Scott his job, and replacement Lou Holtz went 0–11 the next year.

But Holtz was a coach with a national profile, having won a national championship at Notre Dame. He never quite took the Gamecocks to that level, but he got the program turned in the right direction, and he did it quickly. The Gamecocks went 8–4 in 2000 and 9–3 the next year. They won the Outback Bowl in each of those two seasons and were ranked in the top 20 at the end of both years.

Holtz never found that kind of success again at South Carolina. The best the Gamecocks could do was 6–5 in 2004, and that season ended on a sour note. South Carolina was invited to the Independence Bowl, but it refused to accept the offer. The Gamecocks punished themselves after getting into a brawl with Clemson toward the end of a 29–7 road loss. Clemson also turned down a bowl bid. Holtz stepped down a few days later in a move that ended his coaching career. Then South Carolina made a hire that took the Gamecocks to the next level.

SKIPPING SKIP?

When Lou Holtz stepped down as the South Carolina coach after 2004, he was replaced by Steve Spurrier shortly afterward. But was that supposed to be the case? Former Gamecocks assistant coach Skip Holtz said that an agreement was in place for him to replace his father as the South Carolina head coach. But the school went in a different direction and hired Spurrier.

Steve Spurrier is congratulated by his players after defeating Florida in 2010.

5

THE PRESENT AND THE FUTURE

THE SOUTH CAROLINA FOOTBALL TEAM WAS LOOKING TO HEAD IN A NEW DIRECTION AFTER LOU HOLTZ STEPPED DOWN AT THE END OF 2004. THE GAMECOCKS HAD A COMBINED RECORD OF 16–19 THE PREVIOUS THREE YEARS. THAT LEFT THE ATHLETIC DEPARTMENT LOOKING FOR SOMEONE TO LIGHT A FIRE UNDER THE PROGRAM.

South Carolina quickly focused on Steve Spurrier, the former national-title-winning coach at Florida coming off of a disappointing run in the NFL. Spurrier wanted to get back into the college game, and South Carolina seemed to be the right spot. The two sides soon agreed to a long-term deal.

Spurrier was thrilled because the job offered him a new challenge. The Gamecocks had only the 1969 ACC title and nothing else of major significance in the trophy cabinet. Spurrier had won that national title at Florida and was hoping to do the same at South Carolina.

"That's one of the big reasons I thought it was the perfect place," Spurrier said. "I want to go somewhere they haven't done a whole lot so we can get in uncharted waters, do some things that have never been done."

And Spurrier did accomplish some of those things in Columbia. His Gamecocks teams regularly made it to bowl games—missing only once in 10 seasons. They got a foothold in the national top 10 and beat some of the toughest teams in the country. And despite never winning a national title, climbing the ladder in the difficult SEC was a big accomplishment in itself.

JADEVEON CLOWNEY

Jadeveon Clowney, one of the most fearsome defensive players in school history, terrorized SEC quarterbacks from 2011 through 2013. He was surprisingly quick for a guy who was 6-foot-6 and 274 pounds. He registered 24 sacks and nine forced fumbles with the Gamecocks, and he used his big frame to stuff the run as well.

Clowney made all the highlight reels with one of the biggest hits of the 2012 season. In the fourth quarter of the Outback Bowl, Michigan led by a point and had the ball near midfield. Running back Vincent Smith took a handoff, but Clowney met him head-on six yards behind the line of scrimmage. Smith's helmet went flying as he coughed up the ball. Clowney recovered the fumble, and the Gamecocks went on to win. The Houston Texans made Clowney the first overall pick of the 2014 NFL Draft, making him the first Gamecock to go No. 1 overall since George Rogers in 1981.

Jadeveon Clowney was a big hit against Michigan at the Outback Bowl.

Spurrier was named the SEC Coach of the Year for leading the Gamecocks to a 7–5 record in his first season. The team set a school record by winning five straight conference games. During the streak, they won at Tennessee for the first time ever. They also beat Florida for the first time since the 1930s.

Another milestone victory for Spurrier was a 16–10 win against No. 4 Mississippi in 2009. That was just the second time in school history that South Carolina had beaten a top-5 team. Linebacker Eric Norwood had a huge game for the Gamecocks under the lights at Williams-Brice

WINNERS AT LAST

Steve Spurrier did something that no other coach had done at South Carolina. He truly made the Gamecocks a winning program. They did not have a losing record in his 10 full seasons as head coach. They finished at 6–6 in 2007, the only season South Carolina did not have a winning record or make a bowl game. They finished above .500 for seven straight years, matching the longest streak in school history from 1928 to 1934. Plus, the Gamecocks won 11 games in a season for the first time, and they did it three years in a row.

Stadium that night. He finished with two sacks, 10 tackles, and a partially blocked punt.

Things really started to click for Spurrier and the Gamecocks in 2010. The highlight was their victory over No. 1 Alabama, which sparked a run to the SEC East Division title. Spurrier again was picked as the SEC Coach of the Year for leading the squad to a 9–5 record.

That turned out to be Spurrier's best year, as the Gamecocks didn't win another division title during his reign. But they did go 11–2 with New Year's Day bowl victories in each of the next three seasons.

The next year South Carolina slipped to 7–6, and things got even worse in 2015 when the Gamecocks stumbled to a 2–4 start. They were beaten badly by Georgia and LSU, and Spurrier decided to call it quits after the sixth game. After assistant coach Shawn Elliot finished out a dismal 3–9 season, the Gamecocks went to another former Florida coach to replace Spurrier.

In 2016 Will Muschamp was picked to be the 28th head football

Will Muschamp stands by as his team prepares for kickoff in a 2017 game against Vanderbilt.

coach in school history. Muschamp had developed a strong reputation as an assistant coach at LSU, Auburn, and Texas. But he struggled in his first experience as a head coach, a four-year stint with the Gators. Muschamp knew that replacing a legendary coach would not be easy. But he said Spurrier was a big help through the transition.

"He has been a guy that, in my time at Florida and in my time at South Carolina, has really been positive in supporting me, and I appreciate that," Muschamp said.

Jake Bentley directs traffic during the Gamecocks' comeback win against Michigan in the Outback Bowl.

Muschamp slowly began moving the Gamecocks back to where they had been during Spurrier's best times. They finished with a 6–7 record in 2016 and made it to the Birmingham Bowl, where South Florida defeated the Gamecocks 46–39. The season's highlight was a 24–21 victory over No. 18 Tennessee at Williams-Brice Stadium in late October.

The Gamecocks posted a 9–4 record in 2017, Muschamp's second year. Two of the losses were against the No. 2 and No. 4 teams in the nation, Georgia and Clemson, respectively. Sophomore quarterback Jake Bentley started all 13 games and threw 18 touchdown passes. Their success earned them a spot in the Outback Bowl, where they rallied from a 19–3 deficit to beat Michigan 26–19. Bentley threw two touchdown passes in the comeback. He hit Bryan Edwards from 21 yards out and then threw a 53-yard strike to Shi Smith to put South Carolina on top for good.

School officials appeared happy with Muschamp's work during his first two years as talk of a contract extension began to surface. Muschamp had taken a lot of heat at Florida, especially for the team's offensive struggles. But at South Carolina, he received praise for helping to reestablish recruiting connections in the region. In early 2018 it remained to be seen how far Muschamp could take the Gamecocks, but the winning tradition appeared to be in good hands.

TIMELINE

1892
The South Carolina football program begins with a loss to Furman.

1906
School trustees ban the football team over the behavior of its spectators.

1907
Gamecocks football returns to stay in Columbia.

1922
The Gamecocks join the Southern Conference.

1934
Carolina Stadium opens. The name changes nearly 40 years later but it remains South Carolina's home.

1980
Senior George Rogers runs for 1,781 yards and 14 touchdowns and wins the Heisman Trophy.

1983
Joe Morrison takes over as head coach and guides the Gamecocks to three bowl games in his six years on the job.

1991
South Carolina joins the SEC.

1994
In their ninth try, the Gamecocks finally win a bowl game, defeating West Virginia 24–21 in the Carquest Bowl.

1999
Lou Holtz takes over as head coach.

South Carolina goes to its first bowl game, losing to Wake Forest 26–14 in the Gator Bowl.

1946

Paul Dietzel becomes head coach at South Carolina, eight years after winning the national title at LSU.

1966

The Gamecocks win the ACC championship.

1969

South Carolina leaves the ACC and plays independently until 1991.

1971

Carolina Stadium is renamed Williams-Brice Stadium.

1972

Steve Spurrier replaces Holtz and becomes the most successful coach in South Carolina history.

2005

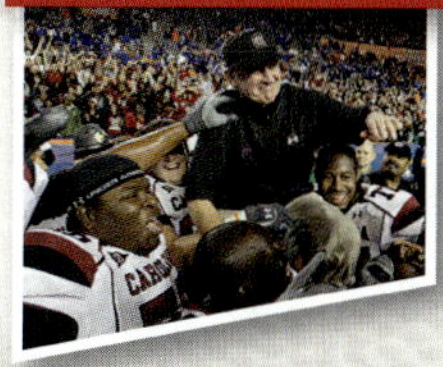

The Gamecocks beat No. 1 Alabama and go on to win the SEC East Division title.

2010

Spurrier resigns as head coach six games into the season

2015

Will Muschamp steps in as head coach and goes 6–7 in his first year, taking the Gamecocks to a bowl game while rebuilding the program.

2016

The Gamecocks improve to 9–4 with a win over Michigan in the Outback Bowl.

2017

QUICK STATS

PROGRAM INFO*
University of South Carolina, 1892–

OTHER ACHIEVEMENTS
ACC championships: 1
Bowl record: 9–13

HEISMAN TROPHY WINNER
George Rogers, 1980

KEY PLAYERS
(POSITIONS, SEASONS WITH TEAM)
Brandon Bennett (RB, 1991–94)
Todd Ellis (QB, 1986–89)
Stephen Garcia (QB, 2008–11)
Harold Green (RB, 1986–89)
Alshon Jeffery (WR, 2009–11)
Marcus Lattimore (RB, 2010–12)
Kenny McKinley (WR, 2005–08)
George Rogers (RB, 1977–80)
Sterling Sharpe (WR/RB, 1983; 1985–87)
Steve Taneyhill (QB, 1992–95)

KEY COACHES
Steve Spurrier (2005–15)
86–49–0; 5–4 (bowl games)
Jim Carlen (1975–81)
45–36–1; 0–3 (bowl games)
Lou Holtz (1999–2004)
33–37–0; 2–0 (bowl games)

HOME STADIUM
Williams-Brice Stadium (1934–)

*statistics through 2017 season

QUOTES & ANECDOTES

The routine remains the same before each home game. The South Carolina football team is dropped off on the Garnet Way in Gamecock Park. They then walk through crowds of fans with the Carolina Marching Band until they reach the locker room.

Steve Spurrier was known for his ability to poke fun at himself and others. He certainly didn't stop doing that when he resigned as the South Carolina football coach midway through the 2015 season. Spurrier, 70 at the time, made it very clear that he was simply stepping down from the job. He said he might coach again. Or maybe not. Or maybe he was just not sure. But Spurrier made it clear that no matter what, his time with South Carolina was over. "I'll just be the former head ball coach now," Spurrier said at the press conference where he stepped down. "It's time for me to get out of the way and let somebody else have a go at it."

George Rogers was happy he won the Heisman Trophy in 1980. He also won a Super Bowl in January 1988 with Washington despite not playing much in that game. But when it comes to college, he wanted more in football than just the trophy. "I'd give the Heisman Trophy back to get a National Championship, to be honest with you, because that's how much my team means to me," Rogers said in 2010.

GLOSSARY

All-American
Designation for players chosen as the best amateurs in the country in a particular sport.

athletic director
An administrator who oversees a school's coaches, players, and teams.

conference
A group of schools that join together to create a league for their sports teams.

coordinator
An assistant coach who is in charge of the offense or defense.

draft
A system that allows teams to acquire new players coming into a league.

extra point
A kick worth one point attempted after a touchdown.

line of scrimmage
The place on the field where a play starts.

recruiting
Convincing a high school player to attend a certain college, usually to play sports.

rival
An opponent with whom a player or team has a fierce and ongoing competition.

sack
A tackle of the quarterback behind the line of scrimmage before he can pass the ball.

FOR MORE INFORMATION

ONLINE RESOURCES

Booklinks
NONFICTION NETWORK
FREE! ONLINE NONFICTION RESOURCES

To learn more about the South Carolina Gamecocks, visit abdobooklinks.com. These links are routinely monitored and updated to provide the most current information available.

BOOKS

Kendall, Josh. *100 Things South Carolina Fans Should Know & Do Before They Die.* Chicago, IL: Triumph Books, 2013.

Wilner, Barry. *The Story of the College Football National Championship Game.* Minneapolis, MN: Abdo Publishing, 2016.

Wilner, Barry. *Total Football.* Minneapolis, MN: Abdo Publishing, 2017.

PLACE TO VISIT

Williams-Brice Stadium
1125 George Rogers Boulevard
Columbia, SC 29201
803-777-4202
gamecocksonline.com/facilities/williams-brice-stadium-new.html

Williams-Brice Stadium has been South Carolina's home stadium since 1934. The original name was Carolina Stadium before the estate of Martha Williams-Brice gave money that helped expand the building. The name was changed in 1972.

INDEX

ABOUT THE AUTHOR

Jeff Seidel has been a journalist in the Baltimore-Washington area for more than 30 years. He lives there with his wife, two children, and two very faithful cats.